ideals COUNTRY

50 Years of Celebrating Life's Most Treasured Moments

Vol. 51, No. 4

*"Now I yearn for one of those old, meandering, dry,
uninhabited roads, which lead away from town . . ."*

Henry David Thoreau

IDEALS—Vol. 51, No. 4 June MCMXCIV IDEALS (ISSN 0019-137X) is published eight times a year: February, March, May, June, August, September, November, December by IDEALS PUBLICATIONS INCORPORATED, 565 Marriott Drive, Suite 800, Nashville, TN 37214. Second-class postage paid at Nashville, Tennessee, and additional mailing offices. Copyright © MCMXCIV by IDEALS PUBLICATIONS INCORPORATED. POSTMASTER: Send address changes to Ideals, PO Box 148000, Nashville, TN 37214-8000. All rights reserved. Title IDEALS registered U.S. Patent Office.
SINGLE ISSUE—$4.95
ONE-YEAR SUBSCRIPTION—eight consecutive issues as published—$19.95
TWO-YEAR SUBSCRIPTION—sixteen consecutive issues as published—$35.95
Outside U.S.A., add $6.00 per subscription year for postage and handling.

ISBN 0-8249-1118-0

Cover Photo, RED BARN, Dick Dietrich Photography
Inside Front Cover, BOY IN TUB, Frances Hook
Inside Back Cover, BARBER SHOP, Richard Hook

D1716807

The Road

Margaret Williams Stevens

It dips in shadowed grace below the rise
Where ageless trees form archways overhead,
Then crestward climbs from out its darkling bed
To cleave the ragged rocks which rim the skies.
Its trail gives glimpse to wooded paradise
As, wandering, the highway's serpent bed
Curves narrow to the gravel way ahead
And plunges deep to hear the wood thrush cries.

Red sumac fringe and berries juicy black—
No super-highway rivals beauty here.
With aim, yet aimlessly, it takes you back
To childhood's gay abandon held so dear.
Then sounds again the junction's roaring track,
And yesterday is just an atmosphere.

Opposite Page
COUNTRY LANE
Bristol, Maine
Dick Dietrich Photography

SUNFLOWER GOLD

Erma Elder Hallmark

Sunflowers, tall and leafy,
Along a country lane,
Supported by a wire fence,
Lush from recent rain—
Heavy with their blossoms,
They look up to the sun,
Waiting to sleep gently
When the day is done.

"One I love, two I love,
Three I love the same;
Four I love with all my heart":
I play the old-time game
Until, full-circled, empty,
Life's final fortune's told,
And in the scattered petals
I stand in solid gold.

Summer in the Country

Gail Brook Burket

He soon forgets neat playground rings and slides,
    With fields and woods inviting him to play.
His memory grows sweet with scores of rides,
    Perched high upon tall loads of clover hay.

He finds wild raspberries and feasts at will
    With cheerful thrush and catbird coteries.
He races to the top of every hill
    And makes a game of climbing low-branched trees.

He soon discovers streams where he can wade
    On sun-warmed pebbles while the hours stroll by
And stretches then upon grass-cushioned shade
    To watch white thunderheads meringue the sky.

But best of joys he loves remembering
    Is soaring skyward on a grapevine swing.

Morning Cloud

Virginia Blakemore Moody

How far above the misty, dreaming veil
You float aloft with light and fleecy sail
When first the lark has caroled morning song,
And balmy winds make swift your way along.

The moon has left its towering perch above,
Its task fulfilled for those who are in love,
And leaves you now to reign as one supreme
While you await the sunlight's searching beam.

No menace lies within your bosom now,
No darkened fringe or frown upon your brow.
You weep not for the sighing flower or tree;
Your magic carpet floats entirely free.

You flaunt your matchless beauty from the sky
While far below you dewy meadows lie.
Ah! Morning Cloud! I greet you and extol
The splendor you accord the eye and soul!

SHUSH-BE-TOU LAKE
White Mountains, Arizona
Dick Dietrich Photography

Lure of the Desert

Harriet Leila Rourke

Endless trails in the desert
  Lure the wanderer on his way,
The roving spirit of a gypsy lad
  At the close of another day.

Wind-blown shrubs are beckoning
  As the sun is sinking low
And casting beams of radiant light
  With rainbow tints aglow.

The vast expanse of sand dunes
  Grips the soul like a magic hand—
The night bird's call, the cricket's chirp,
  The heat of burning sand.

Waning light at eventide
  Fades in the crimson west,
And silence gently spreads her robe
  O'er a desert scene at rest.

10

Grandpa's Stories

Dorothy Brownfield

As I'd come to the end of a childhood day,
    A happy but tired little chap,
The best time of all was the moment when I'd
    Climb up in my grandpa's lap.

Sturdy and tall and snowy-haired,
    He'd smile down at me and say,
"Well, Boy, what kind of a story
    Shall I spin for you today?"

His eyes would grow soft then and dreamy,
    And I knew he was living again
Those long-ago days on the prairies—
    Golden days, when a cowboy he'd been.

"There was one time I remember well.
    It was while we were driving up cattle.
Cap, my faithful old shepherd dog,
    Was riding behind my saddle.

"I was missing a glove when we got home;
    Must have dropped it along the trail.
Old Cap trotted back and fetched it for me.
    Never did know that dog to fail.

"My best horse? Recollect that was Trixie.
    What a beauty, that coal-black mare!
On the Fourth of July we led the parade.
    She and I sure made a pair,

"Dressed all in buckskin, fringed and beaded.
    Oh, how the band did play!
We were prancing high, while the flags were flying.
    I tell you, Boy, that was a day!"

Thrilled by his tales, I'd close my eyes
    And imagine me there by his side,
Riding the trails and facing the dangers
    Back when the West was wild and wide,

Cooking over an open campfire,
    Sleeping out under the stars so near,
Up at dawn from my saddle-pillow,
    Trailing a herd of bawling steers.

"Those were the best days," my grandpa says,
    And I reckon they had to be.
I'm glad he lived then and remembered well
    And can pass his tales down to me.

Generation Gap

Delphia Frazier Smith

A lad wished he were older,
A really grown-up man;
He'd go to work each day—
Do things his daddy can.

Dad looked so wistfully
At Grandpa in the shade
And wished he could retire;
Grandpa sure had it made!

Grandpa was just thinking,
As he looked for his cane,
How he'd like to travel back
And be a boy again.

FATHERS

Author Unknown

A father is a thing that is forced to endure childbirth, without an anesthetic.

A father is a thing that growls when it feels good—and laughs when it's scared half to death.

A father never feels entirely worthy of the worship in his child's eyes. He's never quite the hero his daughter thinks, never quite the man his son believes him to be, and this worries him, sometimes. So he works too hard to try and smooth the rough places in the road for those of his own who will follow him.

Fathers grow old faster than other people. They have to stand at the train station and wave good-bye to the uniform that climbs aboard. And while mothers can cry where it shows, fathers stand there and beam outside—and die inside. Fathers have very stout hearts, so they have to be broken sometimes or no one would know what's inside of them.

Fathers are what give daughters away to other men who aren't nearly good enough so they can have grandchildren who are smarter than anybody's.

They hurry away from the breakfast table, off to the arena which is sometimes called an office, a workshop, or a farm. There, with cal-loused, practiced hands they tackle the dragon with three heads: Weariness, Work, and Monotony. And they never quite win the fight, but they never give up.

Knights in shining armor—fathers in shiny work clothes—there's little difference, as they march away to work each workday.

BITS & PIECES

The most important thing a father can do for his children is to love their mother.

Theodore M. Hesburgh

When I was a boy of fourteen, my father was so ignorant I could hardly stand to have the old man around. But when I got to be twenty-one, I was astonished at how much the old man had learned in seven years.

Mark Twain

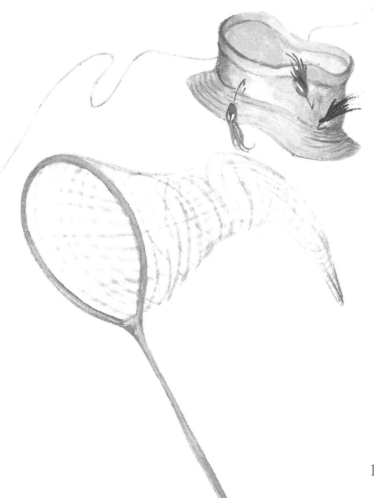

The child is father of the man.

Wordsworth

It is a wise father that knows his own child.

Shakespeare

It is impossible to please all the world and one's father.

La Fontaine

How many a father have I seen
A sober man, among his boys,
Whose youth was full of foolish noise.

Alfred, Lord Tennyson

Honour thy father and thy mother: that thy days may be long upon the land which the Lord thy God giveth thee.

Exodus 20:12

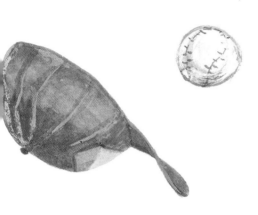

There's a wide-eyed little fellow
    Who believes you're always right,
And his ears are always open,
    And he watches day and night.
You are setting an example
    Every day in all you do
For the little boy who's waiting
    To grow up to be like you.

Author Unknown

A little boy laughs over all sorts of things,
Puppy dogs, engines, and spiders on strings,
But there's probably nothing that pleases him more
Than seeing his daddy come in at the door.

Emily Rose Burt

A SLICE OF LIFE

—— Edgar A. Guest ——

A Boy and His Dad

A boy and his dad on a fishing trip—
   There is a glorious fellowship!
Father and son and the open sky,
   And the white clouds lazily drifting by,
And the laughing stream as it runs along
   With the clicking reel like a martial song,
And the father teaching the youngster gay
   How to land a fish in the sportsman's way.

I fancy I hear them talking there
   In an open boat, and the speech is fair;
And the boy is learning the ways of men
   From the finest man in his youthful ken.
Kings, to the youngster, cannot compare
   With the gentle father who's with him there.
And the greatest mind of the human race
   Not for one minute could take his place.

Which is happier, man or boy?
   The soul of the father is steeped in joy,
For he's finding out, to his heart's delight,
   That his son is fit for the future fight.
He is learning the glorious depths of him,
   And the thoughts he thinks and his every whim,
And he shall discover, when night comes on,
   How close he has grown to his little son.

Oh, I envy them, as I see them there
   Under the sky in the open air,
For out of the old, old long-ago
   Come the summer days that I used to know,
When I learned life's truths from my father's lips
   As I shared the joy of his fishing trips—
A boy and his dad on a fishing trip—
   Builders of life's companionship!

Edgar A. Guest began his illustrious career in 1895 at the age of fourteen when his work first appeared in the Detroit Free Press. *His column was syndicated in over 300 newspapers, and he became known as "The Poet of the People."*

A Father's Prayer

General Douglas MacArthur

Build me a son, O Lord, who will be strong enough to know when he is weak and brave enough to face himself when he is afraid, one who will be proud and unbending in honest defeat and humble and gentle in victory.

Build me a son whose wishbone will not be where his backbone should be, a son who will know Thee and that to know himself is the foundation stone of knowledge.

Lead him, I pray, not in the path of ease and

comfort but under the stress and spur of difficulties and challenge. Here let him learn to stand up in the storm; here let him learn compassion for those who fail.

Build me a son whose heart will be clear, whose goal will be high, a son who will master himself before he seeks to master other men, one who will learn to laugh yet never forget how to weep, one who will reach into the future yet never forget the past.

And after all these things are his, add, I pray, enough of a sense of humor so that he may always be serious yet never take himself too seriously. Give him humility so that he may always remember the simplicity of true greatness, the open mind of true wisdom, the meekness of true strength.

Then I, his father, will dare to whisper, "I have not lived in vain."

Dads and Daughters

Reginald Holmes

Whole volumes have been written
Of fathers and their sons.
Why must daughters and their dads
Be such forgotten ones?

There are special ties that bind
A daughter to her dad
And a certain kind of feeling
That sons have never had.

She goes to Dad for counsel
When things get out of hand.
She knows he has the answers,
That he will understand.

From him she gets her courage;
She thrives upon his praise
And sometimes takes advantage
Of his kind, loving ways.

With due respect to Mother,
Today I'm proud and glad
To write a little poem about
A daughter and her dad!

A Little Boy's Pockets

LaVerne P. Larson

A little boy's pockets—what do they hold?
  Dozens of treasures more precious than gold:
An old rusty knife with a very dull blade;
  A piece of green glass looking like jade;

A key sadly bent that won't fit any lock;
  An intricate part of an old broken clock;
Marbles, some gum, a bit of string, too;
  One bottle cap of a beautiful hue;

The foot of a rabbit, a little seashell;
    Some bark of a tree, a tiny red bell;
A little lead soldier, some thick rubber bands;
    A stamp and two coins from far distant lands;

Part of a map all tattered and torn;
    A whistle of tin quite battered and worn;
A frog or a snake he has captured himself;
    And six shiny pennies add to his wealth.

With all of these treasures, he's rich as two kings;
    A little boy's pockets are marvelous things.

FOR THE CHILDREN

ARTWORK BY RUSS FLINT

CHILDHOOD
Author Unknown

When birdsongs and hens fill the barnyard air
　　And from byre there comes the lowing,
When mist on the hills is rising fair,
　　All the little feet are going.

The game of tag and the bare pony ride,
　　The boat on the water gleaming,
The peat fire of evening and tale beside
　　Fill daytime till bedtime dreaming.

O God bless the girl and God bless the boy;
　　No ragwort-whip may they merit,
And as they grow, be they filled with Thy joy;
　　Thy kingdom may they inherit.

The unique perspective of Russ Flint's artistic style has made him a favorite of Ideals *readers for many years. A resident of California and father of four, Russ Flint has illustrated a children's Bible and many other books.*

28

Lemonade

Nanci Roth-Natale

The lemonade froths,
Liquid sunshine cooling on my tongue,
Condensation rivulets down the sides of the pitcher
Leaving rings on the old table
On the back porch of the old house.
Sweetly scented of summer, it attracts
The boys, thirsty from humid days
Of running and digging and imagining
All the thoughts the world has to offer.
Greedily, they drink and dream.
Seated upon the old porch swing,
Their minds wander in brotherly camaraderie,
Contemplating white clouds in blue sky,
Cooling off with lemonade and shade —
Summer, the season for children.

SUMMER SOLARIUM
Jessie Walker Associates

Happy Birthday, USA

Veva Lewis

You've felt the wheels of progress
    All across your prairie breast;
You've blazed a path of glory
    From your east coast to your west;
You've welcomed every stranger
    Who has stepped upon your shore;
You've aided those less fortunate
    For two hundred years, or more.

You've seen the prairie schooner
    Fade into the western sun;
You've felt the steel of railways

Strung across you by the ton;
Then the ribbons of your highways
    Have unrolled from shore to shore
To transport and feed your children
    For two hundred years, or more.

You've sent your own to succor
    The oppressed of other lands,
And to the ones in trouble
    You've extended open hands;
You've acknowledged God above you
    As your pilot and your oar,
And you've prospered by His blessings
    These two hundred years, or more.

May the children of your future
    Cast their lot on Freedom's side;
May they keep the Constitution
    That has stood against the tide
Of bad times and of rebellions
    Which have knocked upon your door;
Then this country will protect them
    For two hundred years, once more.

HARGREAVES 76

FOR YOU, O DEMOCRACY!

Walt Whitman

Come, I will make the continent indissoluble,
I will make the most splendid race the sun ever shone upon,
I will make divine, magnetic lands
With the love of comrades,
With the life-long love of comrades.

I will plant companionship thick as trees along all the rivers
of America, and along the shores of the great lakes, and all
over the prairies;
I will make inseparable cities with their arms about each
other's necks
By the love of comrades,
By the manly love of comrades.

For you these from me, O Democracy, to serve you,
For you, for you I am trilling these songs.

TRAVELER'S *Diary*

Patricia A. Pingry

STATEOF LINCOLN. The Lincoln Memorial, Washington, D.C. Photograph by Ed Cooper.

The Lincoln Memorial
Washington, D.C.

A visit to the Lincoln Memorial in Washington, D.C., is not a trip to just another monument; it is a journey to America's past, a pilgrimage to a national icon.

"Let us readopt the Declaration of Independence, and with it, the practices, and policy, which harmonize with it."

The Memorial, designed by Henry Bacon, is classic, reminiscent of the Parthenon in ancient Greece. As I slowly climb the steps, looking up at the outer Doric columns, I think it could be set down on the Acropolis with no one the wiser. I marvel at the size of these columns as I walk through them, each forty-four feet high and almost seven and one-half feet in diameter. The thirty-six columns stand guard outside the great chamber, representing, as they do, the thirty-six states of the Union at the time of Lincoln's death. That thirty-six states survived the War Between the States to mourn his passing is due only to the tenacity of the man represented inside who would not let the nation split.

"If we do this, we shall not only have saved the Union; but we shall have so saved it, as to make, and keep it, forever worthy of the saving."

Inside the great chamber, the eight Ionic columns, each five and one-half feet in diameter, rise fifty feet into the air. The chamber is vast, sixty feet by seventy-four feet, with most of its white Indiana limestone walls enveloped in shadow. On the south wall is a stone tablet chiseled with the text of the Gettysburg Address. With this speech, which took no more than seven or eight minutes, Lincoln transformed the country from separate, independent states into one nation.

"Four score and seven years ago our fathers brought forth on this continent, a new nation, conceived in liberty, and dedicated to the proposition that all men are created equal."

Carved into the north wall is a second stone tablet inscribed with the complete text of the Second Inaugural Address of March 4, 1865. Lincoln knew the war was drawing to a close, and his purpose was not to dwell on the past but to look to the future and to healing.

"With malice toward none, with charity for all, with firmness in the right as God gives us to see the right, let us strive on to finish the work we are in, to bind up the nation's wounds, . . . to do all which may achieve and cherish a just and lasting peace among ourselves and with all nations."

It is warm in Washington in June but cool within the shadows of the great chamber. Straight ahead of me rises the figure of the president sculpted by Daniel Chester French. One must experience in person the magnificence of the seated president, sculpted in white marble and gloriously illuminated, to comprehend the enormity of emotion the statue evokes. Lincoln is seated and looking straight ahead toward the Washington Monument. If the statue rose to its feet, it would be twenty-five feet high. Sitting, the statue is nineteen feet high from head to toes.

I think of other statues of presidents I have just seen in Washington. I have seen Thomas Jefferson standing, perhaps about to speak; a marble George Washington in the style of a Greek god; and Andrew Jackson astride a horse. The Lincoln statue seems more like us. He looks like he just sat down, placing his arms firmly on the chair arms and his feet flat on the floor. But that was Lincoln's style, wasn't it? His vision was always further than those around him. His demeanor was simple, belying the intelligence that hid behind the homely guise. And his feet were always anchored in reality: the reality of war, slavery, and a nation torn asunder.

"We shall have so saved it [the Union], that the succeeding millions of free happy people, the world over shall rise up, and call us blessed, to the latest generations."

Turning to go, I look out upon the same view the marble Lincoln has from its chair. It looks out upon the long Reflecting Pool that reaches to the Washington Monument. Beyond the Washington Monument is the Capitol, site of both tirades against Lincoln and praises to honor him. If the statue could turn its head to the right, it would see the memorial to President Jefferson south of the Washington Monument. And if it could turn left, looking north of Washington's obelisk, it would see the White House, Lincoln's last home.

". . . we cannot dedicate—we cannot consecrate—we cannot hallow—this ground. The brave men, living and dead, who struggled here have consecrated it, far above our poor power to add or detract. . . . It is for us the living, rather, to be dedicated here to the unfinished work which they who fought here have thus far so nobly advanced."

The Lincoln statue, since its dedication in 1922 by President Harding, Robert Todd Lincoln, and main speaker Dr. Robert Moton (who was not allowed a seat on the platform but took his seat in the section reserved for African-Americans) has looked out upon temporary buildings set up on the Mall in preparation for a second world war. It has seen Marian Anderson lift her powerful voice in song while sheltered within the shadows of its facade; and it has seen Martin Luther King, Jr., stir thousands with his words.

Walking toward the Reflecting Pool, I marvel at our good fortune that a man as humble yet as shrewd as Abraham Lincoln sat in the White House when he was most needed by his country. President Lincoln was born in a log cabin, but his likeness now resides in a structure fit for an ancient god, a memorial dedicated to a man who gave us a national identity and pointed us toward the road to unity. I suspect he would say our work has just begun.

"It is rather for us to be here dedicated to the great task remaining before us . . . that this nation, under God, shall have a new birth of freedom—and that government of the people, by the people, for the people, shall not perish from the earth."

INDIAN HEAD PENNIES. Photograph by Dusty Willison, International Stock Photo.

Pennies

Although most Americans pay little attention to the change jingling in their pockets, our coins provide a symbol of the liberties of our national heritage. Each coin represents a tangible piece of American history, a history of our ancestors and their struggle to build this great nation. The history of the American penny, for example, takes us back to the beginning of our United States immediately following the revolutionary war.

One of the first laws passed by the newly formed Congress in 1792 was to establish the first official United States Mint in Philadelphia. The following year the mint began issuing the copper Large Cent, the crude design of which caused quite a stir. The obverse or "face" side featured the Head of Liberty, but unfortunately it was so poorly rendered by designer Robert Birch that some claimed she appeared to be "in fright." The chain ring on the reverse side included fifteen links, which represent-ed the fifteen states. The American people, however, saw the chain as a symbol of captivity instead of a symbol of newly won freedom. The public demanded a new design—twice. The first revision included a wreath in place of the chain, but the Head of Liberty still left a lot to be desired. The third design of the Large Cent is known as the Liberty Cap and featured a more elegant portrait of Liberty. Despite its humble beginnings, the Large Cent is now prized by numismatists, or coin collectors, everywhere.

Up until 1858, mints issued specially made coins called *proofs* solely for dignitaries to present as gifts. Collectors especially prize proof coins, which are painstakingly minted, resulting in "flawless gems" with mirrorlike images. Numismatists protested the mint's selectiveness until the Mint Director relented in 1858, and coin collectors too could order proof sets directly from the Treasury Department. Between 1858 and 1915, the mint issued frosted head proofs, in which the head design showed the

Seated Liberty, Liberty Head, or Indian Head with a frosty matte appearance while the background was mirrorlike.

Close inspection reveals that the portrait on the bronze Indian Head cent, minted from 1859 to 1909, does not resemble an American Indian much at all, except that it is dressed with the Indian war bonnet. The story goes that a group of American Indians were touring the mint the same day that coin designer J. B. Longacre's daughter Sarah was visiting. When a chief placed his feathered headdress on Sarah's head, Longacre sketched her portrait, from which he later designed the new coin.

During the Civil War, many citizens saved their money, which quickly resulted in a shortage of coins. In 1863 Indian Head tokens were produced by private citizens in order to relieve this monetary emergency. These coins were accepted as real despite key differences such as "Not One Cent" on the reverse side and the conspicuous absence of the phrase "United States of America." The tokens were soon outlawed when the government made it a penal offense to issue this type of substitute.

In a letter addressed to the Secretary of the Treasury of President Lincoln's cabinet, Pennsylvania minister N. R. Watkinson expressed concern over the lack of religious meaning in the design of the country's coins. Reverend Watkinson wanted to remind United States citizens of the presence of the Heavenly Father in their daily lives. Secretary Salmon P. Chase recommended the phrase "In God We Trust," which was then added to the design of the new two-cent coin issued in 1864. The phrase first appeared on the one-cent piece in 1909 (the Lincoln penny) and became mandatory on all coins in 1955.

The Lincoln cent that we know today was first issued in 1909 in celebration of the 100th anniversary of Abraham Lincoln's birth. Lincoln's portrait on the cent was taken from a plaque designed by Victor David Brenner, a famous Lithuania-born sculptor. The plaque was so well-received that Brenner was commissioned to design the one-cent piece. Brenner included his initials on the early strikes of the coin, causing a public outcry. Mint directors quickly eliminated the designer's mark. A

1909 Lincoln penny bearing the initials VDB is valued higher than a regular 1909 cent.

Another notable Lincoln penny is the 1943 issue. Because copper and nickel were in great demand during World War II, the government changed the composition of the Lincoln penny from copper to zinc-coated steel. These wartime cents were produced only in 1943.

An interesting phenomenon called "double-die" occurred on a limited number of Lincoln cents in 1955. All of the letters and numbers on the obverse side of these coins appear double. While this occurrence is blamed as a mint error, the coin is not labeled a freak and is recognized by all numismatists as a highly prized item.

The Lincoln penny changed again in 1959 with the celebration of the 150th anniversary of the great Emancipator's birth. Mint engraver Frank Gasparro designed a new reverse side for the coin featuring the Lincoln Memorial.

Today's United States penny bears the phrase *e pluribus unum*, Latin for "one out of many." In 1795 the colonists included the phrase on the gold five-dollar coin. Later, they included it in the Great Seal of the United States, and it is required by law today to appear on every United States coin. *E pluribus unum* represents one nation comprised of many states, a reminder of our nation's commitment to the democratic principles on which it's built.

Coins are graded in seventy categories that range from basal state, meaning badly worn and barely identifiable, all the way up to mint state, meaning glittering like a fine jewel. Numismatists take care to keep their coins in prime condition.

Because copper is a soft metal, copper coins bruise and dent easily. Collectible coins should be stored separately from each other and kept clean and dry. Coins that are tucked away in a jewelry box or the bottom of a cookie jar will corrode and discolor, which will lessen their potential worth considerably. Valuable coins should be kept in professional cases made especially for coin collectors.

The humble penny minted today may not purchase much, but collectors delight in the richness of its history and its symbolism of our American heritage.

Handmade Heirloom

Penny Rugs

Patricia A. Pingry

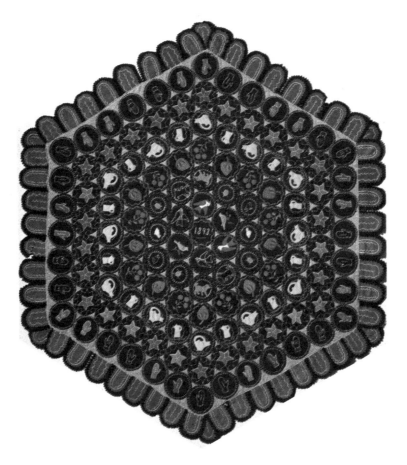

PENNY RUG. Courtesy of the Shelburne Museum, Shelburne, Vermont. Photograph by Ken Burris.

The first penny rug I ever saw consisted of orange circles stitched on a sickly green piece of felt with ragged, uneven blanket stitches around each circle. The term "penny" could well have meant the value of this poor example of stitchery.

The next example I saw, however, was an artistic blend of subtle and warm colors with additional designs added to the center of the piece which gave the feel of an Early American Sampler. These are the wonderful penny rugs that are challenging to make and add a charming heirloom to any home.

Penny rugs are not really rugs in the classical sense; they were originally used as table runners or decorative mats for the table

although there are accounts of some having been used on the floor. They can be of various sizes or even of any base shape: whatever best fits the size and design of the table. (If I were ever ambitious enough to finish one, I think I'd hang it on a wall both to display it and to protect it from spills or footprints!)

The history of the penny rug is somewhat vague, but by most accounts it first appeared in homes in the mid- to late 1800s. Some writers attribute them to frugal seamstresses who did not want to waste a scrap of material. Other writers point to the practice of matching and coordinating color in practically all of the older penny rugs and conclude that they were originated purely for decoration and not from any frugality on the part of the seamstresses. Whatever the reason, these beautifully executed craftworks are suitable for handing down to succeeding generations.

To create a penny rug, you must first determine the finished size and shape desired, allowing for extra fabric for hemming. The fabric for the rug base is usually wool felt or some other tightly woven wool fabric that will not easily ravel. Determine your design using circles and any other designs you would like to incorporate. Choose the colors you want for the design and purchase the additional wool felt or, again, tightly woven wool fabric.

Cut out your templates from cardboard using pennies, quarters, or even silver dollars to trace around. Also cut out any special design you want to include. Then carefully cut your wool, following your design.

Pin and stitch as you might for an appliqué, except center the smallest circle on top of the next largest circle. With heavy cotton thread in contrasting colors, sew a blanket stitch around the smaller circle, attaching it to the larger circle beneath. Center these circles over the largest circle, pin, and work the blanket stitch around the medium-sized circle, attaching it to the largest. Once all of the circles are stitched, lay out the circles and any additional design pieces over the wool base, pin each, and sew a blanket stitch around each piece, much as you would for an appliqué.

Very creative stitchers may choose to work embroidery into the smallest of the circles. In order to personalize the penny rug, one may use designs of herbs or flower blooms for a gardener, various styles of fountain pens for a writer, or babies' names and birthdates for a doting grandmother.

After all of the pinning, appliquéing, and blanket stitching have been finished, the only thing left to do is fold over the hem, press to the wrong side, pin, and blindstitch, catching the fabric underneath the pennies. Giftwrap, hang, or place on a table.

Penny rugs have been gracing the table-tops of American homes since the 1800s, but they are not as common as other works of needlecraft seem to be. Now that I am attuned to this craft, however, I am seeing them more frequently. Penny rugs make a lovely diversion from quilting or cross-stitch, and when subdued shades of wool are used, they add an Early American style to a home's decor. The next time you contemplate throwing out old woolen skirts, men's suits, or blankets, consider making a penny rug before pitching the clothes in the trash. After all, a penny rug saved is a penny rug earned.

Know'st Thou America

Victor E. Southworth

Know'st thou America, where we from every land
Unite in friendly fellowship, all evil to withstand?
Where freedom of the people forever reigns supreme?
Where we together labor to render real our dream?

Know'st thou America? We call the world to see
The greatness of America that is and is to be!
Know'st thou the glory of what we can achieve
When we for one another in liberty believe?
When human worth stands foremost, the chiefest of all good,
And democratic principle is clearly understood?

Know'st thou America? With spirit unconfined
In joyous self-surrender we stand for humankind!

LEGENDARY AMERICANS

Lisa C. Thompson

Marian Anderson
Concert Contralto

The stellar singing career of Marian Anderson began at age six when she joined the Union Baptist Church junior choir in her hometown of Philadelphia. Soon she was singing solos; and by age eight, she was even performing for other neighborhood churches, who billed her as the "ten-year-old contralto." Anderson sang in her church's adult and junior choirs for seven years, often filling in for soprano, tenor, and even medium baritone parts when needed. Anderson credited her strong background in church music for giving her the solid foundation she needed to become a professional musician.

Marian Anderson was born in South Philadelphia in 1902 to John and Anna Anderson. When her father died in 1912, Anderson moved into her grandmother's house with her mother and two sisters. Anna Anderson's income as a department store cleaner barely supported the family, and Marian Anderson vowed to herself that one day her mother would no longer have to work.

While Anderson was still in high school, the famous African-American tenor Roland Hayes was invited as a guest soloist at Union Baptist Church. Anderson was asked to sing on the same program; and Hayes was thrilled by her deep, rich contralto voice and soon recommended her to several concert organizers in the city. What little money she made from these performances, Anderson used to help support her family. She knew she needed voice lessons to develop her technique but could not afford them.

A blessing arrived in the form of Anderson's high school principal, Dr. Lucy Wilson. Dr. Wilson arranged for Anderson to audition for the prominent vocal coach Guiseppe Boghetti, a stern Italian who was highly selective of his students. At the audition, a nervous and jittery Marian Anderson stood before Boghetti. When she finished singing the Negro spiritual "Deep River," Boghetti said, "I will make room for you right away." A benefit concert, which included a performance by Roland Hayes himself, reaped more than enough money to pay for an entire year of lessons.

Soon after Anderson graduated from high school, she embarked on her first concert tour, traveling to churches and schools throughout the South. Her first big break came in 1923 when she won the chance to perform with the Philadelphia Orchestra in a vocal contest sponsored by the Philharmonic Society of Philadelphia. This success prompted Anderson to take a risk that ended poorly; she financed her performance at New York City's esteemed Town Hall. Disappointed by the small audience, Anderson did not sing her best. When a newspaper review labeled her performance as mechanical, Anderson returned to Philadelphia depressed and remained nearly silent for months.

Anderson's strong will and determination returned the day her mother came home from work sick and feverish. Despite her mother's objections, Anderson promptly informed her mother's boss that Anna Anderson had resigned. She decided to return to her singing career and make enough money so that her mother would never need to work again.

After more performances and lessons with Boghetti, Anderson won a competition sponsored by the National Music League. Her prize was the opportunity to perform with the New York Philharmonic Orchestra. After a splendid performance, she received a rave review from the *New York Times*. During the next few years, Anderson traveled to Europe to study and perform and thus began her huge success overseas.

When Anderson returned to the United States, she had signed with the successful impresario Sol Hurok. One of her first engagements back in the states was to perform at New York City's Town Hall—the very site where she had failed eleven years earlier. This performance, however, was much different. The reviews agreed that Anderson was a magnificent contralto.

In 1936 Anderson sang at the White House at the invitation of President and Mrs. Franklin D. Roosevelt. The impression Anderson made on the first lady proved to be invaluable two years later when Anderson found herself the center of a highly publicized controversy.

In 1938 Hurok felt it was time for Anderson to sing at Constitution Hall, Washington's most prestigious auditorium. Repeated attempts to book a date, however, were stifled with the same excuse: the hall was booked. Baffled, Hurok asked a pianist friend to call about the same dates for himself; they were available. Finally, Hurok learned that the owners of the hall enforced a policy which prohibited African-American performers. Outraged, Hurok promptly informed the press, which in turn sent the nation in an uproar.

When Eleanor Roosevelt learned of this, she encouraged the Secretary of the Interior to invite Anderson to give a free public recital at the Lincoln Memorial. With characteristic dignity, Anderson sang on Easter Sunday, April 9, 1939, to a sea of spectators that stretched from the steps of the Memorial back to the Washington Monument. Her heart and soul poured out to the audience through her beautiful voice; and in turn, America deemed Marian Anderson a heroine for justice. Anderson finally sang at Constitution Hall in 1964, and despite the heated dispute of years before, she performed with her usual grace.

Years after that momentous occasion, in 1955, Anderson fulfilled a lifelong dream—performing with the Metropolitan Opera Company of New York City in the role of Ulrica in Verdi's *The Masked Ball*.

Anderson received many honors in her lifetime, including honorary doctorate degrees from universities such as Princeton and Northwestern. She was appointed a United States delegate to the United Nations by President Dwight D. Eisenhower in 1958. She sang for the inaugurations of Eisenhower and Kennedy. Before his death, President Kennedy nominated Anderson for the Presidential Medal of Freedom, which she received just a few days after singing at his funeral.

From her beginning as a poor schoolgirl in a South Philadelphia church choir to her farewell concert at Carnegie Hall, Marian Anderson captured the hearts of all who heard her. Vincent Sheean wrote, "To say farewell to Marian Anderson will not be easy for the American people. Rain or shine, war or peace, she has been with us now for thirty years as a living part of the national consciousness, the voice of the American soul." Marian Anderson died in 1993, leaving behind the legacy of a magnificent American spirit.

Country Church

Craig E. Sathoff

The country church upon the hill
    Is made of white-washed wood.
Its lofty steeple has a bell
    That calls the neighborhood.

The thankful country folk come forth
    In calico and lace
With lifted hearts and peaceful minds
    To seek their meeting place.

What deep fulfillment touches all
    Who come to worship there,
What joy of voices joined in song,
    What comfort found in prayer!

I hear the piano's joyful notes
    Sing sweetly through the hills;
I see again the pianist's hands
    Lend flourishes and frills.

I live again my Sunday School
    With lessons to be learned,
With memory verses to recite,
    And perfect marks to earn.

The caroling at Christmastime,
    The ice-cream socials too,
The picnics for the Sunday School —
    Once more they live anew.

I always visit when I can
    That white-framed church of old.
Its wooden arms have years of love
    And fellowship to hold.

Opposite Page
COUNTRY CHURCH
Jonesport, Maine
Gene Ahrens/FPG International

Readers' Reflections

The Old Hayloft

Golden shafts of sunlight
Slip through the weathered mow,
Waking boyhood memories
Almost forgotten now.
I stand here reminiscing
Amidst the dancing dust
As good old days grow young again
Here in the old hayloft.

Barefoot boy in blue jeans
With muscled, sun-tanned arms,
Hayseeds caught in tousled hair
From working 'round the farm.
I'd wash, after my labor,
Out in the cattle trough,
Then play, swinging on the hay rope,
High in the old hayloft.

Sundays on the creek bank
I'd lie stretched in the sun,
Then follow home the fence posts
And count them just for fun.
But with the coming sunset
I'd once again climb up
To view the pink and salmon sky
From out the old hayloft.

Now pigeons perch on rafters,
Indifferent and aloof,
Mindless of the sentiment
Stored 'neath this timeworn roof.
But my heart holds a treasure
Those tender years have wrought,
In silver threads of memories
Wound through the old hayloft.

Lon Myruski
Washingtonville, New York

Nature's Prayer

A wild rose with larkspur grows
Beside the trail I trod;
Its fragrance softly rides upon
A gentle breeze from God.

I stop to take its beauty in
And notice by and by
That next to it some amethysts
In royal splendor lie.

This tiny altar nature built
O'er centuries of time
Sits still with quiet dignity,
A testament sublime.

J. A. Willi
Bloomer, Wisconsin

The Pinewood Walk

Today I walked beside the pines
Along a path that gently winds
Around a hilly curve and then
Suddenly straightens out again.
On to shady lanes ahead
My feet on Mother Earth did tread.

The pines stood silently and still
With friendly fragrance the air to fill.
On I strolled beyond the bend,
Not caring where the trail would end.
The evergreens, the towering pines,
Led me on between their lines.

An old short stump stood by the way.
"Come sit awhile," it seemed to say.
"Of course I shall," I said aloud
And thanked it kindly as I bowed.
All my cares and woes of day
One by one did fade away.

I looked up toward the evening sky
To watch the birds so gracefully fly
Their skyward paths from tree to tree,
Their wings outspread, so free, so free.
Here and there I paused to touch
A trunk, a limb, the bark, and such.

At last I turned to trace my steps
When evening duties called.
Beneath a pine I almost wept,
I still was so enthralled.
I stopped to kiss one old pine tree
And blessed his heart for cheering me.

Jessie Killingbeck
South Lake Tahoe, California

Birdsong at Twilight

An oriole sang from the old apple tree.
I knew by his song he was singing to me,
For the full-throated tones of his gay roundelay
Sent the worries and cares all frisking away.

So I watched and I listened, and to my delight,
He alighted quite near me, and without any fright
Continued his melody, soaring and trilling
Each clear ringing note, as though he were willing

To share his God-given voice with the world;
His aria spread like a banner unfurled.
And when the last echo had gone with the breeze,
This colorful messenger had with such ease

Restored to my heart what I thought had been lost;
And courage and cheer came again, and the cost?
Just a moment to listen and then to have heard
A miracle worked by the song of a bird.

Ida Helen Fiske
Brooklyn, Connecticut

Editor's Note: Readers are invited to submit unpublished, original poetry for possible publication in future issues of Ideals. Please send copies only; manuscripts will not be returned. Writers receive $10 for each published submission. Send material to "Readers' Reflections," Ideals Publications Inc., P.O. Box 148000, Nashville, TN 37214-8000.

Old Barn

Roy Z. Kemp

It leans a bit as aged things do,
Deserted now by horse and cow;
Its stall doors open, roof aslant,
And emptied now of scythe and plow,
Redolent with the scent of beast,
Of musty straw and rotted hay,
Of cattle feed, of farming things—
So much in use another day.

Its occupants are buzzing wasps
And busy swallows with gray breasts
Who earnestly build stucco homes—
Their small and hardened mud-daubed nests.
It well remembers younger days,
The days it filled a greater need.
But things grow hoary, old, and worn,
And Nature's edict each must heed.

WEATHERED BARN
Warrensville, North Carolina
Gene Ahrens Photography

Country CHRONICLE

Lansing Christman

I have always lived in the country, and it is in the country that I celebrate the glory of June. I feel that I belong to these hills and valleys and flatlands that feature the composition of the countryside; that I belong to their brooks and streams, their songs and music, their peace and serenity.

June, of course, is the month that draws the line between spring and summer. I like to think that the year, like a person, loses some of its youthfulness in June, that it becomes more of an adult, ready to assume the role of maturity. The seasons themselves depict life, from childhood to teen years and on to adulthood. June brings the year to its prime.

June brings other changes too. Perhaps you will hear fewer birdsongs now that summer is here, as the birds are engaged in their nesting chores. Fewer carols, trills, and melodies fill the air; but if you listen carefully, there are still some birds who will grace you with a song. I listen dreamily to the coo of the mourning dove, the mimicking song of the mockingbird, the whistles of the meadowlark and cardinal. The bobwhite calls out to stake its claim to this spot or that as its territory, not to be tampered with nor disturbed. The dawn bears the serenity of summer, a little more subdued than the jubilant springtime dawn.

As I go walking in the fields, I sense the steady pulse of the year. I watch the ripening hay across the hills undulate in the gentle wind. I breathe deeply the sweet aroma of new-mown hay in a nearby meadow.

What I see and feel and hear today in the country will forever be a part of me, clear and pure as the summer brook that nurtures the cress and marigold. I feel my Creator close to me; I can sense my hand in His as He leads me on to seek the peace and contentment that He bestows so generously upon the hills and mountains and valleys, these places we call ours during our tenancy on earth.

The author of two published books, Lansing Christman has been contributing to Ideals *for over twenty years. Mr. Christman has also been published in several American, foreign, and braille anthologies. He lives in rural South Carolina.*

Canning with Neighbors Is Fun

For some people the ideal vacation means camping in the mountains, visiting a big city, or spending a few weeks by the sea. But the vacation a Scotswoman living in Boston thinks will be the most enjoyable this summer is one it took wartime restrictions to bring about. She wants to stay on a farm in Vermont and can food in one of the seventeen community canning centers to be opened in the state about July 15.

The speed with which both the woman and her husband, a lawyer, decided that putting up fruits and vegetables with a dozen other people would be more fun than seeing New York plays or relaxing on a sunny beach still surprises them. He had been describing a cosy cottage for rent on the ocean front not far from Boston, where he could commute throughout the summer, when she suddenly said, "No, let's not take it. Wouldn't you like to visit the Hardy farm in Vermont again? Besides," and the awareness of a newly discovered idea came into her eyes, "I think I'd like to can at the center."

The lawyer with a lively interest in what goes on about him is likely to try his hand at canning too on their vacation. And he won't lack for masculine company among the busy workers, pressure cookers, baskets of garden stuff and tin cans. Sixty-four rugged Vermont men, who are more accustomed to eating the "vittles" than preparing them, came regularly to the centers during the canning season last year.

Vermont is only one of the many states throughout the Union where community canning centers with modern equipment and instruction by trained teachers will be offered free or at exceedingly low rates this summer.

Although Vermont has one of the smaller canning programs (Maine had about fifty centers last summer with an enrollment of 6,000, and tiny Rhode Island with its forty-five centers attracted 16,000 canners), the equipment and procedure the Scotswoman of Boston found in the St. Johnsbury center are typical of most. She relates: "We started out one morning in the milk truck. Mr. Hardy, the farmer, was driving, with another city woman sitting beside him, and Mrs. Hardy and I tucked away in the back of the truck with our bushel baskets of corn, beets, and carrots stowed about us. It was pretty windy, but we managed to hang on until we reached the center, which was formerly a laundry.

"Inside, Mrs. Hardy registered with a secretary and explained that my friend and I were visitors from the city. We bought tin cans at four cents each, or two dozen for eighty-five cents, and made appointments to use the electric corn-cutter for half an hour at a time.

"We washed the vegetables in a huge sink, cut the corn, and I went downstairs to cook them on gas-burner plates. When the food was cooked, we rinsed the cans with cold water, put the name of the owner and the type of food on each, and filled them. Then we dropped them into a steam bath and left them there for a specified time.

"After we had clamped the covers on the cans with an electric tin can sealer (that was fun, too!), we turned them over to two men who put them into very large pressure cookers. When they were thoroughly done, the men took them out with "fishnets" and cooled them in cold water.

"We started at noon and had put up one hundred cans by four o'clock. The work was so easily

CANNING DAY. Archive Photos.

done and the staff of five people were so helpful that we felt as if it were a new kind of social. Afterward we felt so fresh we went calling for a couple of hours."

Over 22,000 householders and victory gardeners in the New England states enjoyed this "new kind of social" last summer, and discovered too the value of community cooperation on more projects. Working together in 275 centers, they donated part of the vegetables, fruits, and meats they canned for school lunches and welfare purposes. In Maine, one pint out of five, or 99,194 pints in all, were left for the school lunch program. As a result of the interest widely aroused in conserving food and planning better meals through the educational program, the Maine Parent-Teachers' Association plans to sponsor an extensive school lunch program in the elementary grades.

So thoroughly has community canning taken hold of millions of men and women that its postwar prospects, unlike those of many other emergency programs, are very good. State canning supervisors are making plans to adjust present programs to peacetime needs, in response to the requests of many canners who have enjoyed the centers' social contacts and profited by the instruction and use of the equipment.

Originally printed in The Christian Science Monitor Magazine, *June 10, 1944.*

Blackberry Summer

Ruth Marie Katchentz

In other times and other years
Berries grew in sweet profusion,
Dark and heavy, hanging low,
Fragrant from their wild seclusion.

So often on a summer's day
I'd climb through rails of meadow fence,
Searching for the dusty fruit
That filled my mouth with succulence.

The sounds of summer circled me
As berries dropped in metal pail,
Cicadas shrilling on the trees,
The plaintive call from hidden quail.

The blackened harvest simmered down
To labeled jars in bright array:
Childhood sitting on the shelf
Collecting dust from yesterday.

BLACKBERRIES
Bristol, New Hampshire
Johnson's Photography

Cherry Picking Time

Loise Pinkerton Fritz

It's cherry-picking time again,
And, oh, what joy it is
To see the ripened fruit hang low,
The bright red fruit, sun-kissed.

Short days ago white blossoms sweet
Bedecked the orchard trees,

And gathering nectar from each bloom
Were neighboring honeybees.

The blossoms now have turned to fruit;
The harvest time is nigh;
How tasty will these pickings be
In tarts, preserves, and pie!

THROUGH MY WINDOW
Pamela Kennedy

Strawberries from Heaven

The front page of the food section in the *Washington Post* carried a color photo of a huge strawberry pie. Plump, red berries rose majestically from a golden crust. I was sold. Rushing to the nearest supermarket, I wheeled my cart to the produce section, ready to load up with luscious, ripe strawberries. There they were, abundantly heaped in a bin bounded by plastic parsley.

Funny, they didn't smell like strawberries. I picked up a few and turned them over. Up near the stem they were white and hard. Under the special supermarket lights they looked red at first, but when examined closely, they appeared to be a sickly orange hue.

"Are these local?" I asked the man stacking cucumbers.

"Nope," he replied.

"Where did they come from?"

"Peru, I think," offered the cucumber man.

"Peru!" I envisioned a plump Peruvian mother strawberry waving good-bye to her unripe youngsters at the pier as they started their long voyage to America. I tossed the handful of berries back. I wanted big, fat, juicy American berries, berries that had ripened to sweet perfection in the humid heat of a Virginia June, berries that had not traveled more extensively than I had!

A few nights later, thumbing through the recreation section of the *Post,* I stumbled upon an article featuring "U-PICK" farms. There were dozens of farms within fifty miles of home where I could pick my own fruit and veggies. I could almost taste that strawberry pie! After considering Summer's Farm, Winding Creek Orchard, and Smitty's Fruit Ranch, I settled on a place that matched my expectations: Nature's Bounty Plantation.

Winding through the countryside on the way to Nature's Bounty, I rolled down the windows and let the fresh country breeze whip through the car. I turned off the main road onto a smaller, curving drive. On my left, rows of deep green berry plants alternated with furrows of rich earth. The sweet scent of crushed strawberries floated through the windows. I smiled, remembering an equally fertile field in the rich alluvial valley of my Washington state hometown—and how I used to sneak berries from my mother's heaping baskets forty Junes ago.

"Will we be able to eat the berries while we're picking?" my daughter asked. I was sure she was imagining sneaking juicy strawberries from my heaping baskets, and I laughed at her grinning anticipation.

"Only if I don't catch you first!"

We parked and gathered up our wooden flats at the edge of the berry field and then headed out to the rows assigned for picking. Kneeling in the damp earth, I plucked a fat, red berry and ate it greedily. Sweet summer juice flooded my mouth. These were strawberries fit for a pie!

We picked for a long time, lost in summer thoughts, content between earth and sky, surrounded by other berry pickers. Now and then my daughter would ask me to examine an especially large berry or to note an abundant red cluster half-hidden under broad green leaves. Her lips and fingers were stained bright pink, and dust clung to her sweaty cheeks. It was a perfect day for picking strawberries, and we couldn't stop. There was such a delicious abundance. Finally, we lugged our loaded flats to the truck for weighing, paid the proprietors of Nature's Bounty, and headed for home.

Back in my kitchen, the counters overflowed with strawberries. We filled bowls and pots and baskets. We gave berries to neighbors and anyone who happened to stop in. We made pies and jam and ice cream topping and froze berries for winter use. I had not planned to have so many, but when you are picking warm berries on a sunny afternoon, it is easy to become intoxicated with abundance. When the pies were in the refrigerator and ruby-hued jars lined my pantry shelves, I felt like the High Potentate of Strawberries.

"Don't you think you overdid it just a bit?" queried my husband, licking a dollop of strawberry jam from his thumb.

"It is impossible to 'overdo' the accumulation of strawberries," I replied indulgently. "Besides, if I have any left over I'm planning to send them to Peru."

Pamela Kennedy is a free-lance writer of short stories, articles, essays, and children's books. Wife of a naval officer and mother of three children, she has made her home on both U.S. coasts and in Hawaii and currently resides in Washington, D.C. She draws her material from her own experiences and memories, adding bits of her imagination to create a story or mood.

RED BARN REFLECTED. Brown County, Wisconsin. Darryl R. Beers Photography.

A Summer Outing

Carole McCray

Splashes of golden apricot paint the daybreak's blue horizon. The harsh tone of an alarm clock is unnecessary for signaling me to rise and shine, as I hear the songs of house wrens greeting the sun. I too share their enthusiasm, as a glorious day is forecast for jaunting along the country backroads with a special friend.

Shared interests bring Connie and me together, namely, gardening, antiques, and natural foods. This day encompasses all our favorite things as we set out to pick our own

60

tomatoes at a nearby farm and then rummage through the countryside antique shops. Weeks earlier, red raspberries, plump as gumdrops, filled our berry boxes. Now with the languid days of summer soon to be a memory, we are eager to make the most of our end-of-summer outing.

I wait for Connie's arrival and ponder the lovely quality of the early hour. Two monarch butterflies perch on the rim of the silver-gray birdbath, and the lush grass is veiled by a canopy of dew. Connie steps onto my sun porch, and we exchange thoughts about the sun-dappled morning. Eager to begin our trek, we then gather our basket lunches, straw hats, and a time-worn quilt to spread on summer's carpet. Our adventure begins.

Meandering country backroads lend themselves to leisurely viewing the unadorned beauty of the rural roadsides. Summer's landscape is sketched in wooden fences and dry walls of pewter-colored stone. Bordering these dividers of the land are creamy fluffs of Queen Anne's lace. Bouquets of pale blue chicory edge the roadsides, while swaying daisies and brilliant black-eyed Susans sweep the fields with color.

The paved road we travel soon turns into a narrow graveled lane. A wooden sign tells us "to honk your horn for picking." Promptly, a sun-tanned girl, with pigtails flying, greets us and leads us to rows of ripe tomatoes. Warmed by the hot sun, we are grateful for the occasional breezes that gently fan us. Gathering the warm tomatoes goes quickly, and we chat about the various ways our bounty will appear at our table through the coming seasons: plum tomatoes for thick sauces on pasta and pizza, stewed tomatoes in soups and savory stews, and tomato juice seasoned with fresh herbs. With our buckets brimming,

Connie and I head down the sunlit path.

With the farmer's permission, we spread our tattered pink quilt under a stately maple. Connie's gazpacho is a refreshing cold soup for the steamy day. Whole wheat and blueberry muffins, juicy nectarines, wedges of sharp Asiago cheese, and herbal iced tea complete our luncheon fare.

Our view of the countryside is inviting. In this tranquil scene sits a cranberry-red barn where two marmalade-colored kittens play inside on the cool, slab floor. The flower gardens are a palette with vibrant blooms of lavender foxglove, pink roses, blue and white delphiniums, and a medley of colorful dahlias bordering the perennials. Near the flower bed, sky-blue morning glories entwine a black hand pump.

On this fine day, the wide country roads beckon us to travel. We journey over a roller coaster road, and its dips and sharp turns draw us closer to some real "finds" at our favorite antique shops. My buy of the day is a large yellowware bowl—perfect for holding an abundance of pink-cheeked peaches, wonderful for cradling dough for rising bread, and ideal for displaying a harvest centerpiece of Indian corn, bittersweet, and tiny gourds on the antique hutch in my kitchen. A spotless bolt of old beige tea toweling striped with a red border catches Connie's attention—placemats, matching napkins, and a tea cozy are on her mind. She decides to buy the entire bolt.

From meadows and woodlands, summer's harvest in rural gardens, and country collectibles in quaint shops, we bring home feelings of contentment and fond remembrances of a lovely June day. An antique bowl, a red-striped tea cozy, and jars of tomatoes lined up on my pantry shelf make me recall a special time, a special find, and a special friend.

Ideals' Family Recipes

Favorite Recipes from the Ideals Family of Readers

Editor's Note: If you would like us to consider your favorite recipe, please send a typed copy of the recipe along with your name and address to *Ideals* Magazine, ATTN: Recipes, P.O. Box 148000, Nashville, Tennessee 37214-8000. We will pay $10 for each recipe used. Recipes cannot be returned.

CHEESY CHICKEN WINGS

In a small bowl, combine ¾ cup crumbled crackers or fine bread crumbs, ¾ cup Parmesan cheese, 1 teaspoon dried basil, ½ teaspoon dried oregano, and ½ teaspoon garlic salt. Set aside. Wash 16 chicken wings and pat dry. Cut each wing into two pieces, discarding the tip. Melt ½ cup butter. Dip each chicken wing in butter and then crumb mixture. Arrange coated chicken wings in lightly oiled baking dish. Bake in preheated 375° oven for 30 to 45 minutes, or until golden brown and crispy. Chicken wings should be tender. Serve warm or chilled.

Gwendolyn Shew
West Terre Haute, Indiana

SPINACH SALAD

In a small bowl, blend 1 cup salad oil, ⅓ cup ketchup, dash salt, ¼ cup distilled white vinegar, and 1 tablespoon Worcestershire sauce. Stir in ½ to ¾ cup sugar to taste. Chill dressing well. In a large bowl, combine one 10-ounce package of fresh spinach, rinsed and drained, one small red onion separated into rings, four hard-boiled eggs, chopped, and ¼ cup bacon bits. Just before serving, pour dressing over salad and mix well.

Gwendolyn Shew
West Terre Haute, Indiana

COUNTRY POTATO SOUP

In a large saucepan, combine 3 cups potatoes, peeled and diced, ½ cup diced celery, ½ cup diced onion, and 1½ cups water. Add 2 chicken bouillon cubes and ½ teaspoon salt. Bring to a boil over medium high heat, cover, and simmer over low heat until vegetables are tender, about 20 minutes. Do not overcook. Stir in 1 cup milk. In a mixing bowl, gradually add 1 cup milk to 2 tablespoons flour, mixing until smooth. Mix in 8 ounces sour cream and 3 tablespoons chopped chives. Slowly stir sour cream mixture into soup. Cook over low heat until thick.

Karen Varney
Middletown, Ohio

Editor's note: For a cool summertime alternative to hot soup, try pureeing the above mixture in a blender or food processor and serving it chilled. Delicious!

ASPARAGUS CASSEROLE

Melt ¼ cup butter or margarine in a small frying pan. Add ⅓ cup slivered almonds and sauté until browned. In a large bowl, combine 1 cup cream of mushroom soup and 2 eggs, beaten. Add sautéed almonds plus dash salt and dash pepper to taste. Sprinkle bottom of buttered 1½-quart casserole dish with ¼ cup fine bread crumbs. Spread two 14½-ounce cans cut asparagus, drained, over crumbs. Pour soup mixture over asparagus and top with another ¼ cup fine bread crumbs. Bake in a preheated 325° oven for 35 to 40 minutes.

Frances Hite
Fargo, North Dakota

TANGY CARROT SALAD

Place 5 cups of thinly sliced carrots in large pot, fill with water to top of carrots, cover, and simmer 10 minutes; drain. In a medium saucepan, combine one 10¾-ounce can tomato soup, undiluted, 1 cup granulated sugar, ¼ cup salad oil, ⅔ cup vinegar, and 1 teaspoon pepper. Bring to a boil over medium high heat, stirring constantly. Cool slightly before adding carrots, 1 large green pepper, chopped, and 1 large onion, thinly sliced and quartered. Mix well, drain, and transfer to storage container. Chill.

Cornelius Hogenbirk
Waretown, New Jersey

Serenity

Gail D. O'Connor

There is an Eden in my past. I love to think of it:
That shallow, effervescent stream; that stony bank, sunlit;
The flat rock in midstream where I lay, content to read
And dream away the long, hot days — I had no other need;

64

FOREST BROOK
South Glastonbury, Connecticut
Fred M. Dole Productions

My picnic lunch, enough to last the afternoon or more;
    The pungent pines; the solitude; the droning insects' snore.
So many childhood hours were spent in that slow-motion way;
    They seem idyllic to me now as I rush through each day.

Oh, to be a child again in summer's lazy haze,
    When books and dreams and bubbling streams inhabited my days.

A Quiet Place

Joy Belle Burgess

I find my every joy is here
Where endless waves of mountains rise
And lift their gleaming, snow-capped peaks
Into the blue ethereal skies;
For I may breathe primeval air
Of forest floor and pungent boughs
Within the dark secluded shade
Of spreading ferns and leafy shroud.

I find my every joy is here
Where litanies are murmuring sweet
From babbling brook and waterfall
That grace the rugged mountain steep;
For I may gaze with dreamful eyes
Where ripples bathe the pebbled shore
And revel in the grand, sweet song
Of melodies unheard before.

I find my every joy is here
Amidst the choirs of singing birds
That lift their wings in graceful flight
And flit among the spreading firs;
For I may hear their notes that float
On every cool and gentle breeze,
The lovely sighing of the wind
That whispers through the towering trees.

I find my every joy is here
Within the forest's green embrace,
Where much of earth and much of heaven
Weave for me a quiet place;
For deep within this hallowed shrine,
His still, small voice my soul can hear
Within the silence of a prayer
When no one but my God is near.

ALWAYS IN TOUCH

Ardis Rittenhouse

Each time I work the soil and sod,
I feel I've touched a part of God.
When flower seeds I plant with care
Come through the ground, I know He's there;
And when I seek the shade of trees,
His breath stirs up refreshing breeze;
And in each shower I find His tears
To wash away my doubts and fears;
And when the sun shines from above,
I'm warmed by His eternal love.
So every night to Him I say,
"Thanks for my share of Your today."

Opposite Page
GARDENING TOOLS
Dan Dempster Photography

From My Garden Journal

by Deana Deck

Lilies

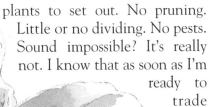

Every once in a while the pleasure derived from gardening seems in danger of being overshadowed by the drudgery and the routine. I sometimes feel that way when a busy spring schedule forces me to squeeze gardening between all the other activities to which I'm committed. It happens in summer too when work and vacation schedules and the garden's need to be weeded and watered are at odds with each other.

I never consider giving up the garden, mind you—just the gardening. I catch myself daydreaming about a work-free, ever-blooming garden. No annuals to start from seed. No bedding plants to set out. No pruning. Little or no dividing. No pests. Sound impossible? It's really not. I know that as soon as I'm ready to trade the rewarding work and constant surprises of a cottage garden for a less demanding landscape, about 200 varieties of lilies are waiting to enter my life.

Actually, I already have quite a few members of this colorful and stately family. I have a lovely stand of Easter lilies (*Lilium longiflorum*) saved from a long ago holiday. Nearby is a bright, ever-expanding group of orange-red tiger lilies (*L. tigrinum*). Rising behind the perennials, where it rules with aristocratic grace, is a colony of fragrant Dragon Strain Orientals that grow nearly six feet tall, producing white blooms edged in magenta. Their smaller companion is a cluster of radiant *L. rubellum* that produces masses of rose-pink blooms in late spring and early summer.

Of the several advantages to the all-lily garden, the most obvious is that you basically plant them and forget them. Another is the possibility of a long-blooming season . Some species are very early spring bloomers, but these are followed by a succession of others that bloom periodically through September. Yet another advantage is that lilies can be grown just about everywhere. All species are indigenous to the North Temperate Zone and many are native to the United States. One additional advantage is that because the plants have few pest problems—field mice and moles are the worst—they'll keep you environmentally friendly; they require (almost) no toxic sprays to get through the blooming season. My kind of plant!

Once lily bulbs are established, an annual early spring feeding with an inorganic 5-10-5 fertilizer followed by another dose just before blooming will keep the bulbs vigorously blooming and spreading by producing multiple "daughters" each year.

LILIES

Authorities advise using inorganic chemical fertilizers on lilies and warn against the use of manure as a nutrient, even when dry and composted, since it aids the growth of disease fungi.

To ensure the best start for lilies, give them a good home: a deep, well-draining bed of loose, rich soil in an area that receives full sun. Dig down about a foot into the soil and mix bone meal, compost, and a small amount of 5-10-5 fertilizer into the bottom two or three inches of soil. Cover this layer with another two inches of top soil and set the bulbs on top of this layer. (Check with a nursery to determine the planting depth for each species of lily; it will vary with the size of the bulb.)

Lilies are most attractive when planted in groups rather than rows. I like to plant several bulbs staggered around the edge of a two-foot circle, which gives them plenty of room to spread.

Unlike most bulbs, lilies get off to the best start when the bulbs are purchased with the roots attached. That means it's best to buy American, because European growers usually remove the roots before shipping their bulbs. Lily bulbs should also be planted before they dry out completely, which is another reason to purchase American bulbs that are dug and shipped more frequently over shorter distances.

Watering is not difficult with bulbs. The objective is to keep them healthy, and too much water will lead to fungus, root rot, and other problems. I find that a soaker hose laid under a thick layer of mulch accomplishes two things: saving water and eliminating weeds. With a soaker hose, water seeps evenly into the root zone, and because it doesn't come into contact with the plant's foliage, mildew and other fungal disease problems are less likely. The mulch conserves soil moisture, as well, thus reducing the amount of water you need to add, and it prevents weed growth. Most weeds require light for the seeds to germinate, which a heavy mulch prevents; and those seeds that do germinate are usually not strong enough, as lily stalks are, to get through the mulch. An exception is Bermuda grass, which can enter the bed by sending out stolons from surrounding areas. Keep a good clean border around your garden to prevent this difficult-to-control problem.

Lilies are for the most part disease-free. If you seek out healthy bulbs and plant them in areas where lilies have not previously been cultivated, they can usually be grown without the need for spraying. There are, however, two diseases to be aware of. One is botrytis blight, which affects and kills young stalks. After the affected stalks are cut and burned, spread of the blight can be controlled with a mild Bordeaux spray—a mixture of copper sulfate and lime.

The other disease is the lily virus, which is spread by plant lice. Plant lice can be controlled with a single spraying of Malathion or Systox in mid-June, hopefully the only time you'll need to use a toxic spray. Choose bulbs that are firm and succulent, showing no signs of damage or rot.

The many different types of lilies include the large-blossomed trumpet varieties, gracefully dropping pendants, upward-facing bowl and chalice types, a reflexed variety with curled back petals, and an open type called sunburst. Lilies are available in sizes to fit every garden plan, from small spring lilies only a few inches tall to others five to six feet tall.

Their blooming seasons are agreeably varied as well. For early June and July blooms, select the Asiatic strains. (Easter lilies only bloom in early spring one time, when they've been forced by the grower. After they're transplanted to the yard they will bloom in summer, like other lilies.) Trumpets, Aurelian hybrids, and early Orientals will bloom in July and August. The most fragrant of the lilies, and the ones that bloom latest in the season, are the many Orientals.

Beautiful, fragrant flowers that require next to no work—that's the garden I fantasize about when I have too much to do and not enough time. If it sounds appealing to you too, start thinking about lilies!

Deana Deck lives in Nashville, Tennessee, where her garden column is a regular feature in The Tennessean.

Marriage Is a Garden

Carolyn Alley

Marriage is a garden;
    You reap what you sow.
If you nourish your seedlings,
    They'll flourish and grow.

Plant potatoes of kindness
    And plain common sense;
Let squash be the damper
    On intolerance.

The greens will bring loving
    And giving and hope;
And onions, persistence,
    To stay with it and cope.

Plant corn there for humor,
    For relish as well,
And berries for sweetness
    To make all things jell.

Add well-chosen spices
    To give life a zing,
Like interests and hobbies
    And doing your thing.

Your practical garden
    Is just about done,
But the true, earnest gardener
    Has barely begun.

Grow flowers for color
    And warmth and romance,
The roses for passion,
    The daisies for dance.

Bulbs are renewal—
    Every year a new spring;
Vines flower with urges
    To both climb and to cling.

Plant in one corner
    An evergreen tree—
Reciprocal trust
    And loyalty.

This is your garden;
    Protect every seed;
Water with sorrows
    And weed well from greed.

Silence will parch it,
    And spite will bring frost;
An ill-tended marriage
    Is easily lost.

But one that is worked in
    Is fertile and deep;
Reap bushels of loving
    To share and to keep.

Opposite Page
ANTIQUE WHEELBARROW
Gay Bumgarner

I Love the Sea

Karen H. Dusek

"Oh, I love the smell of the sea," said she,
As she skipped over sunburnt sand,
"And I love the 'pop' of crisp kelp balloons
As they snap between
heel and land.

"I love the tickle of the sand crab's feet
As it scuttles about in my hand,
And I love the slap of the waves as they lap
Against me
where I stand.

"I love the sight of the lighthouse light
On a high and invisible shore,
As it signals a silent and cheerful goodnight
Against the ocean's roar."

Opposite Page
DAISIES ON THE OREGON COAST
Humbug Mountain, Oregon
Ed Cooper Photo

Ways of Day

Robert Penn Warren

THE FIRST POET LAUREATE OF THE UNITED STATES OF AMERICA

I have come all this way.
I am sitting in the shade.
Book on knee and mind on nothing,
I now fix my gaze
On my small son playing in the afternoon's blaze.

Convulsive and cantankerous,
Night heaved, and burning, the star
Fell. What do I remember?
I heard the swamp owl, night-long, call.
The far car's headlight swept the room wall.

I am the dark and tricky one.
I am watching from my shade.
Your tousled hair-tips prickle the sunlight.
I watch you at your sunlit play.
Teach me, my son, the ways of day.

Opposite Page
COUNTRY KITTEN
Original painting by Donald Zolan

Readers' Forum

Meet Our Ideals Readers and Their Families

MRS. ROCHELLE PLESKO from Burns Lake, British Columbia, wanted to share this photograph of her son Evan feeding neighbor Andrew Midgett's goat. Rochelle and her husband John have three children—Ian, 10, Kerra, 8, and Evan, now 6. They live about an hour and a half from the nearest town, the journey to which includes miles of gravel roads and a ferry boat ride. The Pleskos enjoy water-skiing on nearby Ootsa Lake and tending their garden during the long, warm June days.

Fond of family excursions, the Pleskos last year traveled north of the Arctic Circle to camp and enjoy the wilderness. Rochelle said they had a great time but chose to sleep in the van instead of tents because the insects were large and hungry!

The Pleskos have been married for thirteen years. John is a native Canadian, and Rochelle is an Oregon native. They enjoy reading *Ideals* when John's mother, Elizabeth Plesko, brings along copies from her subscription when she visits.

MRS. BEVERLY TOWNSEND sent us this photograph of her husband Newton with their great-grandson Ian minding the bonfire in the backyard of their Woodburn, Oregon, home. At two and a half years old, Ian is a serious little boy, a real thinker, says Great-Grandma Bev. He lives nearby with his younger brother Codi and their parents Eric and Maria Van Orden. When visiting his great-grandparents, Ian follows "Pappa Newt" around everywhere. They especially enjoy taking care of the scrub jay that has taken up residence in a backyard hedge. Ian named the bird Oliver and loves to talk to him.

When Beverly isn't spoiling her nine grandchildren and five great-grandchildren, she loves to read each issue of *Ideals*—a Christmas present from her daughter-in-law Elsie Townsend.

ATTENTION WHEAT WEAVERS!

The most recent *Thanksgiving Ideals* included a Handmade Heirloom article about wheat weaving. We've received such a positive response to this craft that we want to provide more information to our readers.

For further information on wheat weaving, consult *Wheat Weaving Made Easy* by Carolyn Schultz and Adelia Stucky, Library of Congress Catalog Number 77-79473, Copyright © 1977, Mennonite Press, North Newton, Kansas.

IDA HELEN FISKE of Brooklyn, Connecticut, wanted to share with us this photograph that her daughter Sandra Billings sent to her. After spying the delicious bird seed in the feeder in Sandra's yard, the raccoon pounced on the feeder only to find himself stuck on the line of the pulley. Sandra and her husband Roger live in Grantham, New Hampshire.

Ida visits Sandra and Roger occasionally, but she keeps quite busy at the Pierce Memorial Baptist Home, where she has lived for the past seventeen years. As one of the more experienced residents, Ida presented a program on "How to Handle Aging." She has also presented programs on music, participated in the handbell choir, and quilted more quilts than she can even remember. At age ninety-three, Ida credits her longevity to her active lifestyle.

The youngest of Ida's three children, Sandra, gave Ida a subscription to *Ideals* for Mother's Day. Ida is also proud to be a grandmother of eight, great-grandmother of eleven, and, just recently, great-great-grandmother of one.

Thank you Rochelle Plesko, Beverly Townsend, and Ida Helen Fiske for sharing with Ideals. *We hope to hear from other readers who would like to share photos and stories with the* Ideals *family. Please include a self-addressed, stamped envelope if you would like the photos returned. Keep your original photographs for safe-keeping and send duplicate photos along with your name, address, and telephone number to Readers' Forum, Ideals Publications Inc., P.O. Box 148000, Nashville, TN 37214-8000.*

A CALL TO ALL POETS

For half a century, *Ideals* has been a supporter of poetry by publishing many of the quality poems sent to us each day by our readers. Now, to mark our fifty years of publishing poetry for America, we are searching for "the best anniversary poem."

The poem should relate to an anniversary—a marriage, birthday, or other milestone that is in keeping with the anniversary theme. The winning poem will be featured in the 1995 *Ideals Valentine* issue along with a short biography of the poet. The poet will receive a one-time cash award of $100 for the poem and a plaque commemorating the honor.

To enter, submit only one poem, typed and double-spaced, to **Ideals Anniversary Poem, P.O. Box 148000, Nashville, TN 37214-8000** along with your name, address, and telephone number. Poems will be returned only if a self-addressed, stamped envelope is included. All entries must be the original, unpublished, and sole work of the person submitting the poem. It is the entrant's responsibility to understand and abide by the laws regarding plagiarism and copyright. No employee or relative of an employee of Ideals Publications Inc. will be considered. **Anniversary poems must be received no later than September 2, 1994.**

Send in your poem today and watch for the winning poem in *Ideals Valentine* 1995!

Publisher, Patricia A. Pingry
Editor, Lisa C. Thompson
Art Director, Patrick McRae
Contributing Editors, Lansing Christman, Deana Deck, Russ Flint, Pamela Kennedy, Nancy Skarmeas
Editorial Assistant, Laura Matter

ACKNOWLEDGMENTS

A BOY AND HIS DAD from *WHEN DAY IS DONE* by Edgar Guest, copyright ©1921 by The Reilly & Lee Co. Used by permission of the author's estate. WAYS OF DAY from *SELECTED POEMS 1923–1975* by Robert Penn Warren. Copyright ©1966 by Robert Penn Warren. Reprinted by permission of Random House, Inc. Our sincere thanks to the following authors whom we were unable to contact: Carolyn Alley for MARRIAGE IS A GARDEN; Erma Elder Hallmark for SUNFLOWER GOLD; Reginald Holmes for DADS AND DAUGHTERS; Roy Z. Kemp for OLD BARN; Veva Lewis for HAPPY BIRTHDAY USA; and Victor E. Southworth for KNOW'ST THOU AMERICA.

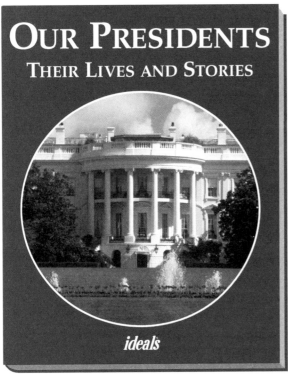